Monographic Journals of the Near East *Afroasiatic Linguistics* 5/4 (September 1978)

ON THE COMPLEXITY OF SOME TYPES OF COMPLEX SENTENCES IN URBAN MOROCCAN ARABIC AND SOME OTHER ARABIC DIALECTS*

by

J. Rosenhouse
The University of Haifa, Haifa, Israel

The complexity of some complex sentence types in Urban Moroccan Arabic is studied here and compared with some other dialects of Arabic. The types are: relative, direct object, subject and (nominal) predicate clauses, and all expansions of NP, and seem to be related both in structure and use (or deletion) of subordinating conjunctions. The variety of sub-classes that exists for the four types, as well as their conditioning, may indicate the complexity involved. Some processes of distinction between structures seem to be developing still, and it is interesting to compare them with earlier stages of Arabic (Classical and Middle Arabic).

CONTENTS

0. INTRODUCTION 2
1. RELATIVE CLAUSES 2
2. DIRECT OBJECT CLAUSES 4
3. SUBJECT CLAUSES 6
4. PREDICATE CLAUSES 8
5. DISCUSSION 9
6. COMPARISON WITH SOME ARABIC DIALECTS 11
7. SUMMARY 12
REFERENCES 15

*The author wishes to thank cordially Dr. B. Ingham from the Department of Phonetics and Linguistics at the School of Oriental and African Studies, The University of London, for reading the manuscript and various suggestions for elucidating some points discussed in it.

0. INTRODUCTION

"Complex Sentence" is the most common term for those sentences where a certain basic function has been expanded into the form of a clause, so that it is embedded within the first basic structure. The embedded part is usually called a "subordinate clause", for it depends in some way on the sentence frame in which it is embedded. Frequently, but not always, the subordinate clause is longer, i.e. is made up of more words than an equivalent phrase structure and has the characteristic structure of a sentence, i.e. a subject and a predicate (which a phrase lacks). A subordinate clause may be introduced by a subordinating conjunction (then it is syndetically subordinated to the main clause) or without such a conjunction (and then it is asyndetically subordinated). Usually there are rules for using either of these two forms of subordination, so that the final appearance of the sentences is not a matter of entirely free choice of the speaker. Other factors that contribute to the final form of the complex sentence are clause order (the main or the subordinate clause at the head of the sentence), word order, verb forms, the adverbs that are used and intonation patterns (which are used in speech, but which are only partly indicated by punctuation marks in the written form of a speech act).

In the present study we shall examine some types of subordinate clauses, namely relative, direct object, subject and predicate clauses representing urban Moroccan Arabic dialects, and we shall try to find the relations between the syntactic structures and the semantic structures of these types of sentences, with their varying degrees of complexity. The study is based on material collected from texts and grammar books of mainly the Moslem communities in Morocco (see Brunot (1931), Colin (1939), Colin (1957), Harrell (1965), Kampffmeyer (1912), Kampffmeyer (1908), Meissner (1905), Mercier (1945), Saᶜid (1958), Singer (1958)) and some recordings of Jewish Moroccan informants now in Israel.[1] The four types of clauses will be presented starting with the relative and direct object clauses and followed by the subject and predicate clauses. This order has been preferred, for the first two types are used in greater frequency than the latter ones, which seems to indicate the primacy of the relative and direct object clauses in comparison with the subject and predicate clauses, and perhaps are also the source from which subject and predicate clauses developed. After discussing these clause types, some comparison with a few Arabic dialects, as well as with Classical and Middle Arabic, will be done, in order to place these structures within a diachronic and synchronic frame.

1. RELATIVE CLAUSES

The relative clause is the expansion of a nominal attribute of an antecedent noun, and thus can be subordinated to any nominal member of the sentence, even to the nominal part of an adverbial complement. In the urban Moroccan Arabic dialect we have found four types of relative clauses defined in terms of their way of subordination as follows:

a. SYNDETIC RELATIVE CLAUSES, in which a definite antecedent noun requires an explicit subordinating particle to introduce the relative clause (*ṣila*, in Classical Arabic), e.g.:

(1) *uma kaibqa ġer ṭṭolba lli kaimšiu fṣṣbaḥ yiqrau* (Kampffmeyer, 1908:25)
'and there do not stay any but the students WHO go in the morning to pray'

(2) *ḫai li ta-iskin f-l-amerik ta-yiḫdim f-s-skuola* (Rosenhouse, Recordings:3)
'my brother WHO lives in America works at a school'

[1]The recordings were made during work on dissertation, see Rosenhouse (1974).

b. PSEUDO-SYNDETIC RELATIVE CLAUSES, where the antecedent is indefinite but forms a nominal phrase group with such words as *wahd-el* 'a, an', *wahad* 'one, someone', *ḥaža* 'thing, something' *ši* 'something, thing', *ʾaḫor* 'another'. The relative clause governed by such antecedents often appears syndetic, e.g.:

(3) *kateᶜref ši waḥed lli yemkellu ysaᶜedni temmak?* (Saᶜid, 1955:92)
'do you know anyone WHO can help me there?'

(4) *ᶜabauna f-l-lil waḥ-l-bato di kan zdid* (Rosenhouse, 1974:57)
'they took us at night in a ship THAT was new'

c. ASYNDETIC RELATIVE CLAUSES, which are governed by an indefinite antecedent (*ṣifa* in Classical Arabic). Clauses where the antecedent forms a nominal phrase group with some attribute as in 1.b above can be included in this group (1.c), if they are asyndetic. See for example:

(5) *kaiḥuṣṣna mōḍaᶜ nbātū fīh* (Kampffmeyer, 1912:119)
'we need a place to stay in (during the night)'

(6) *kant f-iddi waḥd-le-valiža kant tqila bezzaf* (Rosenhouse, Recordings:2)
'I had in my hand a suitcase (which) was very heavy'

d. PSEUDO-ASYNDETIC RELATIVE CLAUSES, in which the antecedent is a "general definition" (*taᶜrīf al-ǧins* in Classical Arabic). In cases with such definition of the antecedent, the subordinating particle is allowed to be used or omitted in Classical Arabic, and this perhaps accounts for the fact that there are also quite a number of "normal" definite antecedents which govern asyndetic relative clauses; for example:

(7) *kēᶜažnūh ūkaiḫalleṭū mᶜâh šṷâi diāl ssᵘkkār dī-kfīhum* (Kampffmeyer, 1908:7)
'they bake it and mix with it some sugar WHICH is sufficient for them'

(8) *ušâf hädâk elṷeld ezzin dịâlu mâ hûṷa ši kâ'in* (Meissner, 1905:59)
'and he saw that boy whose beauty is not be be found'

Besides these structures, relative clause structure was used, even in Classical Arabic, to express what can be described as "causal clauses" (see Spitaler (1962)). They consist of a main clause which is some sort of an emotional exclamation or phrase, such as "thank God", followed by the relative subordinating particle and the clause which explains the cause for the feeling expressed in the main clause. It is clear from the semantic point of view, that the "relative clause" in such cases is not directly governed by the antecedent noun, but rather as though a causal subordinating particle is missing, to complete the sense, as can be seen from the following examples:

(9) *qal-lu lḥəmd llah lli qəlti bdəqmək ləḫrafa kdub* (ᶜAbd al-ᶜĀl, 1968:368)
'he said to him: Thank God that you have said yourself that the story is a lie'

(10) *uhnịa ᶜalêk lli fkkĕk răbbi ᶜala ḫêr* (Brunot, 1931:27)
'and congratulations to you that God has released you safe and well' (a phrase used to a woman after birth)

2. DIRECT OBJECT CLAUSES

Direct Object (= D.O.) clauses are subordinated by syndetic or asyndetic means to the predicate-verb of the main clause. The verb is transitive either of necessity or by choice (some verbs can be used transitively or intransitively freely). D.O. clauses may assume all the possible syntactic forms. D.O. clauses may be classified as to subordination methods as follows (see Rosenhouse (1976)):

group no.	kind of verb	examples	structure in Moroccan Arabic	structure in Classical Arabic
1.	factual	know, agree swear, prove	syndetic/asyndetic	syndetic (*'anna*)
2.	saying	say, think, learn (to know)	asyndetic/syndetic	syndetic (*'inna*/*'anna*)
3.	influence	want, hope, fear, ask	usually asyndetic	syndetic (*'an*)
4.	modal auxilliaries	start, let, permit, hurry, jump, sit	asyndetic + imp. (+*ka*)	asyndetic + imp.
5.	other trans. verbs + *aš*/*ma*	eat, write, do	pseudo-syndetic	pseudo-syndetic
6.	verbs + double d.o.	*bġa*+*h*+fut.	asyndetic imperfect	asyndetic imperfect
7.	verb + double d.o. (1st d.o. formal)	hear, know, see	asyndetic	---

From the comparison with Classical Arabic, which may be considered as background for dialectal developments, it can be seen that the first three groups show the greatest deviation from that base-line. This has happened as a result of the gradual disappearance of the nominalising conjunctions *'inna*, *'anna* and *'an* (used in Classical Arabic for D.O. clauses) from Moslem dialects. In their stead, *bin*, *bayn*, *belli* and *baš*[2] are used for syndetic subordination. However, semantic conditions have also changed, so that the appearance of the D.O. conjunction indicates not merely the syntactical function of the clause, but also an emphasis on the realisation of the action mentioned in the D.O. clause (see Mercier (1945:59)). Such a development has not occurred, it would seem, in the Jewish dialects of Moroccan towns, where *bin*, *baš* etc. are used like *'anna* and *'an* in Classical Arabic. Note this point in the following examples:

(11) *šəhḍo-ᶜlīya bīn ka-nbīᶜ əd-ḍāṛ u-ma-ka-nbīᶜ-ši l-məṣmāṛ* (Colin, 1957:15)
'be witnesses to me THAT I am selling the house and I am not selling the peg'

(12) *bəlḥaqq mni šuft baš kan fiha ssmör bežžāf ... mšit* (Rosenhouse, 1974:66)
'but when I saw THAT it was very cold there ... I went'

(13) *qâlọ li bain ṛâžlĕk bâġi idžụ̄uuž ᶜalîk* (Brunot, 1931:33)
'they told me (=I was told) THAT your husband wants to marry again (lit. 'over you')

[2] *bin* and *bayn* derive from *bi'an*; *belli* < *bi* + *elli* and *baš* < *bi* + *aš*.

(14) *nqūlo hādi dāiza* (Colin, 1957:21)
'let's say (that) that's all right (so)'

(15) *kanhāf ma nžebrek ši fi-ddār* (Kampffmeyer, 1912:5)
'I am afraid I might not find you at home'

(16) *wdābā nḥəbb təmši nʿəndu* (ʿAbd al-ʿĀl, 1968:337)
'and now I'd like that you will go to him'

(17) *kaibdau nnâs isârbo atâi* (Brunot, 1931:37)
'the people start drinking tea'

(18) *ma ʿreftš waš ka-tehḍer belʿarbiya* (Saʿid, 1955:59)
'I did not (do not) know if you speak Arabic'

(19) *ki-nəḥki lkom škūn huwa* (Rosenhouse, Recordings:31)
'I shall tell you who he is'

(20) *wána bīh kandəbbār ma nákul* (Singer, 1958:122)
'and I fix for me with it what to eat'

Some D.O. clauses are indirect questions, and are introduced by a conditional particle (instead of an interrogatory particle), e.g.:

(21) *baš išûf ila fīha ʿâib ulā lla* (Brunot, 1931:53)
'in order to see WHETHER (=if) she has some defect or not'

The examples up to now represent groups 1-5 in the above table. Groups 6 and 7 are involved with "double objects", which are usually governed by the "verbs of heart", as they are called in Classical Arabic grammar. But whereas in Classical Arabic the D.O. clause is syndetically introduced in these cases, in Moroccan Arabic they are asyndetic. To some extent this structure can be considered a substitute for the subordinating conjunction, which as mentioned above, tends to appear more for semantic purposes in the Moslem dialects than for indicating syntactic function. See for instance:

(22) *bġītik tsmaḥ li, ma ngədd ši ngʿod* (Kampffmeyer, 1912:6)
'I want you to forgive me (lit. 'I want you you will forgive me'), I cannot sit down'

(23) *bābâh šāfu mâ ḫrižši min eddâr, qâl ...* (Meissner, 1905:46)
'his father saw him not coming out from the house (lit. 'his father saw him (that) he did not come out ....'), he said ...'

As further development of the structure, the bound pronoun becomes almost an impersonal pronoun (somewhat similar to the *ḍamīr aš-ša'n* in Classical Arabic), so that the D.O. clause functions almost as an apposition to the first D.O., the personal pronoun. The fact that the pronoun is sometimes conjugated to gender and number seems to indicate that the structure is relatively young and not fossil as yet. See the examples:

(24) *ma ʿreftha ʿlaš mšat* (Harrell, 1965:105)
'I did not know why she went away'

(25) *wesmeᶜtu dževwež temmak* (Saᶜid, 1955:105)
'and I heard that he (had) got married there'

There seems to be a special case for the two verbs *ᶜya* 'get tired' and *nsa* 'forget' and the D.O. clauses they govern. Instead of using the imperfect form for the verb in the D.O. clause (as in Classical Arabic) after *'an*, *ma* is used, followed by the verb in the imperfect or the perfect form; this is special, for *ma* in such a *maṣdariyya* function is otherwise almost unused in the dialect. Thus:

(26) *nsīt ma nlbis kiswa sḫōna* (Kampffmeyer, 1912:126)
'I forgot to wear warm clothes'

(27) *ᶜaẏīt ma-nǝ̌fṭǝ̌š ᶜalek* (Singer, 1958:119)
'I have got tired of looking for you'

3. SUBJECT CLAUSES

Subject clauses, like other types of subordinate clauses, can appear at the end of the sentence or after the predicate, and can be syndetic or asyndetic according to structural rules which depend on the semantic and morphological categories of the subject clause, the predicate and the subordinating conjunctions. The major rules for subject clauses in Moroccan Arabic may be summarised as follows:

a. THE PREDICATE PRECEDES THE SUBJECT CLAUSE when:

1) The predicate is a present participle which is fossilised or imperfect fossilised verb forms such as: *ka'in* 'there is', *lazem* 'it is necessary', *yemken* 'it is possible' *ka-iḫǝṣṣo* 'he/it needs, requires'.

2) The predicate is an adverb of place, a demonstrative pronoun, an interrogative particle etc., such as: *hada* 'this', *hnak* 'there', *škun* 'who'.

3) The predicate is a greeting or a "social formula".

4) The predicate is a prepositional phrase (very frequently *ᶜanḍ* and *fi* 'to have').

5) The predicate is negated.

6) The predicate and the sentence where the subject is a clause are involved in the frame of another complex sentence.

b. THE SUBJECT CLAUSE PRECEDES THE PREDICATE when:

1) The relative conjunction (*lli*, *di*, *mǝn*) is at its head and the predicate is not included in any of the groups mentioned in 3a. above.

2) When the subject is emphasised by a syndetic extraposition (through *'amma* 'as to').

3) When the predicate is a clause.

c. THE SUBJECT CLAUSE WILL BE SYNDETIC when:

1) The relative pronoun (*lli, di, mən* etc.) serves as the subject without the antecedent noun; thus the subject can be included in the group of generalising nouns such as "he who, that which, that who, those who". In this way the relative clause becomes a subject clause. This structure is typical of proverbs, generalising statements of wisdom and descriptions.

2) The predicate is a verb which is semantically intransitive and denotes some kind of perception, opinion or mental attitude. This verb is usually a transformation of a transitive verb of perception, and the subject clause of the intransitive verb is the transformation of the direct object of the transitive verb. The subject clause is usually introduced by the nominalising conjunction *baš, bain* (the equivalents of *'an al-maṣdariyya* in Classical Arabic) according to the usage of this conjunction in the dialect (with the Jews more than the Moslems—see above, section 2).

From the above it would seem that ASYNDETIC SUBJECT CLAUSES can be:

1) Those that are not introduced by the relative pronouns (*mən, ma, 'aš, di, lli*).

2) Such sentences where the predicate is one of the modal verb groups (such as *lazem* and *ḫessu* 'it is necessary, he needs').

3) Other verbs which belong to the factual verbs group (see section 2, the table), but are used asyndetically as a specialty of the urban Moroccan dialects.

4) Those sentences where the subject is connected with the predicate through a comparative structure.

Here are some examples of the various types of subject clauses:

(28) *lazem nersel žuž dezzerbiyat mezyanin llᶜa'ila* (Saᶜid, 1955:113)
'I have to send two nice carpets to the family'

(29) *yemkelii nžib mrati weddrari maᶜaya?* (Saᶜid, 1955:42)
'can I bring my wife and the children with me?'

(30) *uhākedâ lli kaidllil kūllu* (Kampffmeyer, 1908:15)
'and thus (is) that who auctions everything'

(31) *škūl lli ṭàḷḷaᶜ had lḥmàḷa?* (Brunot, 1931:73)
'who is this that made this silk belt?

(32) *mbàṛk mᵕsᶜûd ma dzâḍ ᶜandek* (Brunot, 1931:27)
'congratulations for the new born (lit. blessed and lucky (be) what has been added to you)'

(33) *ma fīja mā nākul dāba* (Kampffmeyer, 1912:135)
'I do not feel like eating now—I am not hungry now'

(34) *ẉulli bâqa ṣġẹ̄ṛa ... kaṭᵕbda bᵕṭṭᵕllẹqa* (Brunot, 1931:77)
'and that who is still young (f.sg.), starts with *ṭᵕllẹqa* (a kind of embroidery)

(35) *di ḥfar si ḥāfrā kạ-iṭēḥ fīha* (Brunot-Malka, 1937:169)
'he who digs a pit, will fall in it'

(36) *ḍāhr bein mherrisa fīha ši ḥāža* (Kampffmeyer, 1912:95)
'it seems (looks) that something is wrong (ruined) in it'

(37) *uhadāk əl-qāid, məlli smāᶜa ... tsḥab lo bas hua* (Rosenhouse, 1974:53)
'and that officer, when he heard it ... it seemed to him that it was him'

(38) *uhādi məzyana di kizīu yirauni* (Rosenhouse, 1974:54)
'and it is good that they come to see me'

(39) *ta-ᶜežbni bežžāf nᶜōm fe-ṣṣēfa* (Rosenhouse, 1974:134)
'I like very much to swim in the summer'

(40) *l˘lahúmma, nsījib ṙási mŏn-hād-ĕdğbŏl hsŏn ma iqăṭṭáᶜli ṙási-ṣṣoḷṭån* (Singer, 1958:122)
'O, God, to throw myself from this mountain is better for me than to have the Soltan behead me'

4. PREDICATE CLAUSES

In Arabic the predicate can be a verb, a noun, an adjective or an adverbial phrase; therefore it can also be expanded into a "nominalised" clause. From the point of view of structure, predicate clauses are similar to subject clauses: they may be introduced by the relative pronoun (*lli, di* etc.) when they are "generalised", may open with an interrogatory particle when they are "indirect questions". In the material we checked, they only follow the main-clause subject (unlike subject clauses). Sometimes a personal pronoun appears between the subject and the predicate clause and serves as the copula. Both in such cases and in those where the clause opens with a relative pronoun, the structure seems to be a device for emphasizing the contents of the predicate. See for example:

(41) *ḫūk mn wātāk, ma hū š mn wālāk* (ᶜAbd al ᶜĀl, 1968:308)
'your brother is that who gets on well with you, not that who is your relative'

(42) *ṙā-ana lli nākul jūj!* (Colin, 1957:47)
'it is I who will eat two!'

(43) *u-qālət lo: hā ᶜlāš jīt!* (Colin, 1957:42)
'and she said to him: That is why you have come!'

(44) *kul ši kīf nbğī, lḥamdu llāh* (Kampffmeyer, 1912:36)
'everything is as I want it (= all right), thank God'

(45) *hua di yižbərkom had-si* (Rosenhouse, Recordings:41)
'he is (the one) who will find for you that thing'

(46) *l˘kṭîr mn˘nnâs f˘nnsâ lūmm hiya lli kaṭṙåḍdaᶜ ṷūldha ṷūlla bĕnṭha* (Brunot, 1931:5)
'with many women, the mother is the one who suckles her son or daughter'

We have not found any examples with *baš, bain* etc. introducing the predicate clause. Although this is a possible structure, these conjunctions are only rarely used in Moroccan Arabic (see above, section 2).

5. DISCUSSION

The types presented here look very well organised in their rule-framework: the different clauses are used syndetically or asyndetically in certain formal and semantic circumstances. For relative clauses, however, it would seem that the number of exceptions to the rules (e.g., syndetic relative clauses where asyndetic ones would be expected and vice versa) is too large to be merely mistakes or mixing of structures for prosodic reasons. One assumption might be that this reflects a trend of development which is not as yet stabilised. The trend goes both ways (for relative clauses), from syndetic to asyndetic and from asyndetic to syndetic clause structures. Even in Classical Arabic some freedom was allowed as to the use of syndetic or asyndetic structure in relative clauses, when the antecedent belonged to the semantic category of mass nouns (then its definition by *al* is only formal, actually). These nouns had the semantic features [+general] and [-countable], and thus rather vague (*mubham*) from the aspect of where their "limits" or "edges" are. After examining the examples in question from the Moroccan dialect (and some other Arabic dialects—see section 6, below), we can find that the nouns or noun-phrases involved share this vagueness of definition of the "edges" of the semantic field, even if they do not belong to the category of mass nouns. The unfinished process of extending the category of mass nouns by new members of various degrees of vagueness reflects the complexity of the semantic background of the syntactic rules and their exceptions.

Direct object clauses are basically clear cut, but they become a more complex area on closer examination. Direct object clauses have been classified into four groups (see Rosenhouse (1976)) in accordance with the semantic categories of the verbs governing them, i.e. factual and volitional verbs which govern one D.O. (phrase or) clause, and mental actions and physical actions-verbs, that govern two direct objects, the second of which is a clause. These groups are again divided into two classes each—saying and factual, modal and volitional, verbs of heart and verbs of becoming, 1st form + 2 D.O.s and 2nd and 4th form verbs + 2 D.O.s; and, again, finally, into groups according to whether they are syndetically or asyndetically subordinated. Thus we have sixteen groups of D.O. clauses.

The relation between the first and the second D.O. is sometimes as between a subject and predicate, sometimes the first D.O. is a transformation of an indirect object which has been placed in front of the direct object, and sometimes the D.O. clause is semantically very close to circumstancial clauses, e.g.:

(47) *aš žābik tdīr had šši?* (Kampffmeyer, 1912:37)
'what has made you do it?'

(48) *nṭlub allah nšufek diğja* (Kampffmeyer, 1912:8)
'I ask God for me to see you soon (I pray to God that I shall see you soon)'

(49) *šafetni ka-nešᶜel l-ᶜafya* (Harrell, 1965:259)
'she saw me making (lighting) the fire'

There is also that type of double D.O. which is used probably as a substitute for the subordinating conjunction, which is rarely used in the dialect (as mentioned in section 2, above). All this shows again the variegated semantic substratum which appears as one-type surface structure.

Subject (and also some predicate) clauses use relative and direct object clause structures, as we have seen above, with syndetic or asyndetic subordination following the semantic and syntactic rules relevant to those types of clauses. Still, not all subject clauses can be derived from relative or D.O. clauses: some are expansions of a simple noun-subject (usually a verbal noun). Thus we can tie this aspect of subject clauses (and also of D.O. clauses) with the more general semantic treatment of nominal sentence members in Arabic, that is to say, the *ta'wīl al-maṣdar* 'explanation or expansion of the verbal noun', which in Classical Arabic is usually achieved by preceding *'an al-maṣdariyya* to the subordinated clause, whether it be subject, D.O. or some adverbial clause (preceded by a preposition which forms the subordinating conjunction with *'an*). Relative clauses do not belong to this field, for the relation between the relative clause and the main clause is through an explicit sentence member, the antecedent, with which it has the transformed relation of subject and predicate. However, the other clause types mentioned here are expanded sentence members on their own right, and thus on a different semantic level than the relative ones. We find, then, again, that the label of subject clauses includes various types of clause structures.

There still remains another point to be discussed here—that of interpretation or understanding of certain asyndetic structures, and we shall concentrate here on relative clauses, for in the other cases (D.O., subject and predicate clauses) the position of the subordinate clause in the sentence is sufficient to indicate its function in the sentence. The following examples will illustrate the sort of problems we are dealing with:

(50) *kān wāḥd-əṣ-ṣulṭān ē barrəh el-tlātā de-nnās* (Rosenhouse, 1974:147)
'there was a Sultan (e..) who sent for three men; or: there was a Sultan (e..); he sent for three men; or, a Sultan (e..) sent for three men'

(51) *ḥətta šāfo ši-ġəzlān kā-irᶜāu* (Colin, 1939:1)
'until they saw some gazelles who were grazing; or: until they saw gazalles grazing'

(52) *wsəmᶜit ṣṣōt d-wāḥəd-rrājəl kəyqūl* (ᶜAbd al-ᶜĀl, 1968:358)
'and she heard the voice of a man who said; or: and she heard the voice of a man (while he was) saying'

(53) *kaimšiu lᶜand ši-ṭâlǝb ikṭǔb lha* (Brunot, 1931:7)
'they (would) go to a scholar who will write for her; or: they go to a scholar in order that he may write for her'

(54) *žāb ləᶜdūl yəšhadu ᶜlēh* (ᶜAbd al-ᶜĀl, 1968:347)
'he brought (the) witnesses who will witness on it; or: he brought (the) witnesses in order that they will witness on it'

Example (50) above represents three possibilities of analysis, i.e. coordinate independent asyndetic sentences; a complex sentence with an asyndetic relative clause embedded in it; and a simple sentence with a complex tense (*kān* + perfect form of the main verb). All these are legitimate and grammatical possibilities, so how can one know what the speaker really meant when uttering this sentence? In normal speech conditions one is usually guided by the prosodic patterns, which would be different for each of these syntactic-semantic structures. From the recorded example we hear a slight fall on the word *ṣulṭān* and a level tone on the "hesitation syllable" /ē/ and the rest of the clause, until a slight rise on the word *nās* because of what follows (which is not relevant to the present discussion). Relative clauses in our samples are frequently not detached from antecedents by a pause or a change in intonation, so we are really faced here with the problem of how to explain the falling (end)-tone on the word *ṣulṭān*, if it is the antecedent for the following utterance. Because we have here the long /ē/ which indicates hesitation or uncertainty as to the continuation of the sentence, we may consider this to be a typical structure of mixed patterns:

the beginning of the sentence starts off as a self-contained simple sentence, but after the /ē/ the speaker continues as though it was really a relative clause subordinated to the first part. Such contamination is typical of spoken utterances, not only (or necessarily) of the type of clauses of this specific example. Without the clues from intonation, it would be really an unsolvable problem, and this point can be further demonstrated by the other examples already quoted here.

Examples (51), (52) can be interpreted as either main clause + relative clause or as main clause + circumstancial clause, as the translaitons show. We have here cases of an indefinite antecedent noun followed by an asyndetic subordinate clause which may seem as a relative clause. The form of the verb in the subordinate clause (*ka* + imperfect) is typical of circumstancial clauses, which indicate a static or durational situation, i.e. *al-ḥāl al-muqārina* in Classical Arabic. Although from the point of view of Classical Arabic the word to which the circumstancial clause refers (*ṣāḥib al-ḥāl*) has to be defined, we cannot be satisfied with such a rule, which has its exceptions even in Classical Arabic, for the semantic-syntactic analysis of the modern dialects. Thus, this seems to be another case of one surface structure which is analysable into two deep-structures, which are semantically close but not identical.

Examples (53), (54) deal with a similar problem. Here the nouns *ši-ṭâleb* and *lәᶜdūl* may be considered as antecedents for asyndetic relative clauses (see above, the discussion about phrases with "vague" antecedents, first paragraph of this section); but they can also be considered as introducing the asyndetic purpose clause which can be compared with Classical Arabic *al-ḥāl al-muqaddara* 'the circumstancial clause with a sense of assumption or purpose or directionality'. Here, again, the semantic structure is not clarified by the formal surface structure or by traditional grammar. And as these examples, all four of them, were found in written texts without any indication of intonation and juncture patterns, a definite solution cannot really be suggested for them.

To sum up this section, we have seen that the title "complex sentences" conceals more than the surface structure of main clause + subordinate clause (as against the simple sentence, which comprises only of one sentence structure). The concept complex sentence must obviously be linked to multiple semantic deep level units.

6. COMPARISON WITH SOME ADJECTIVE DIALECTS

To place this study in the frame of Arabic dialects, some comparison with a few of them seems necessary.

One of the earliest recorded periods of dialectal Arabic is Middle Arabic. We rely mainly on Blau (1961) and Blau (1965) which highlight the major trends in Middle Arabic as a whole and not only Jewish Arabic (see Blau (1965, Chapter 1, p. 49). Sections 354-358 and 347 in Blau (1961) refer to various structures of relative clauses, as we have done here. There are examples of "incorrect" relative clauses (that is to say, those that we call here pseudo-syndetic and pseudo-asyndetic clauses) even in Middle Arabic, but it is noted that such examples are relatively rare. The author there remarks that when the antecedent is indefinite but governs a syndetic relative clause, it has a "tone of definition" and a few semantic types of such antecedents are mentioned there. It seems possible to include the examples quoted there within the semantic category of "vague field edges" mentioned above (1st paragraph, section 5).

Direct Object clauses are dealt with in Blau (1961) under the heading "syndetic nominal clauses -'*an*", together with some other subordinated clauses with a nominal function in the sentence structure, including subject clauses, see sections 342-345 there. (Section 345 describes some stages in the development of *bi'an* as a subordinating conjunction also for other clauses than D.O. clauses). Asyndetic D.O. clauses are discussed in sections 334-335, after asyndetic subject clauses (331), predicate clauses (332) and apposition clauses (333). All these structures belong to the chapter "subordinated clauses" in the part on asyndetic clauses. In section 330 the author notes that asyndetic subordinate clauses existed also in Classical Arabic, but there they are rarer than in Middle Arabic. This tendency to use asyndetic subordinate clauses seems to have grown since.

In the modern dialects checked here (Syria, Iraq, Lebanon, Israel (Palestine) and Egypt) the tendency is to continue and develop along the lines shown for Middle Arabic. Thus we see in, e.g. Blanc (1964:127-28), a comparison between Moslem, Jewish and Christian communities the "incorrect relative clauses". This phenomenon is to be found also in Syrian (see Cowell (1964:499), Lebanese (see Feghali (1928:311) and Palestinian (Piamenta, 1966:210) Arabic dialects, but apparently not in the Etyptian dialect (see Mitchell (1962:101), and Spitta-Bey (1880:429-34)).

Direct Object clauses in the Eastern Arabic dialects are usually subordinated, when syndetic, by some derivative form of the classical Arabic *'inna/'anna/'an* (usually sounds *'en* or *'enn*) with or without a suffixed inflected or fossilised personal pronoun. As we have seen, this conjunction has practically disappeared from the Moroccan dialects (and generally from the Maghreb—see Marçais (n.d.:563-64)), while *bain, bin* (their nearest equivalents), *baš* and *belli* (*b* + relative pronoun) have replaced them, sometimes with different conditions of usage. The Iraqi dialect seems to be more like the Moroccan one in this respect than any other of the Eastern dialects checked here, for there, too, *'inn* is practically unused. *'ann* seems to appear only after saying verbs when they mean 'ask for, order' (see Van-Ess, 1918:83)) but *bi'an* appears also (see Weissbach (n.d.:31-34)). Cantineau (1934:238-39) notes that the more characteristic colloquial way of expression in Palmyre for these cases would be the asyndetic subordination, but sometimes the conjunction is used to make perhaps the impression of the more educated "*naḥwiy*" language. The same remark is made by Spitta-Bey (1880:426) about the Egyptian dialect. In the Lebanese dialect, *ṭa* seems to have taken the place of *'an* in many instances (see Feghali (1928:82-83)) for subjunctive subordination, as he calls it, but *'enn* is used similarly to the way it is used in the Syrian or Palestinian dialects.

Subject and predicate clauses are formed according to the different aspects of usage of *'elli* and *'enn* in each dialect, with many examples of asyndetic subject clauses quoted in the sources referred to already.

All these dialects, then, despite their geographical (and sociological) distance from the language and the people who speak Urban Moroccan dialects, and despite differences in details, reflect a basically similar linguistic structure and developmental history ("drift").

7. SUMMARY

We have investigated here both syntactic and semantic relations that exist between four clause types in the urban Moroccan Arabic dialect, namely subject, predicate, object and relative clauses. We have seen that subject and predicate clauses, despite their important status in the sentence structure generally, seem to derive in this respect from object and relative clause structures, which are ordinarily considered as complements or attributes to the main sentence members. The complexity of the relations among these elements can be demonstrated by the following schematic representations.

1. Simple Sentence Members Relations

subject predicate

nom. verbal

adjectival attribute

direct object

any other nominal member

2. Clause Relations (seen by use of the conjugations)

subject , predicate cl.

relative cl. (adjectival)

direct object cl.

(see Fig. 3, following page)

From the comparison with Middle Arabic (Jewish Arabic) we have found that this semantic array appeared at a very early stage, so that the semantics of Classical Arabic did not remain static (except for the written documents of it). As we view the dialects today (at least those that are mentioned here) we can note further individual developments which are still going on, e.g. the change of grouping for synd-tic or asyndetic subordination of relative clauses, the usage of *'an/'anna* according to semantic categories of the governing verb and various substitutes for these conjunctions (two direct objects; *ta*), and the general tendency of increased asyndetic subordination for all of these clause types.

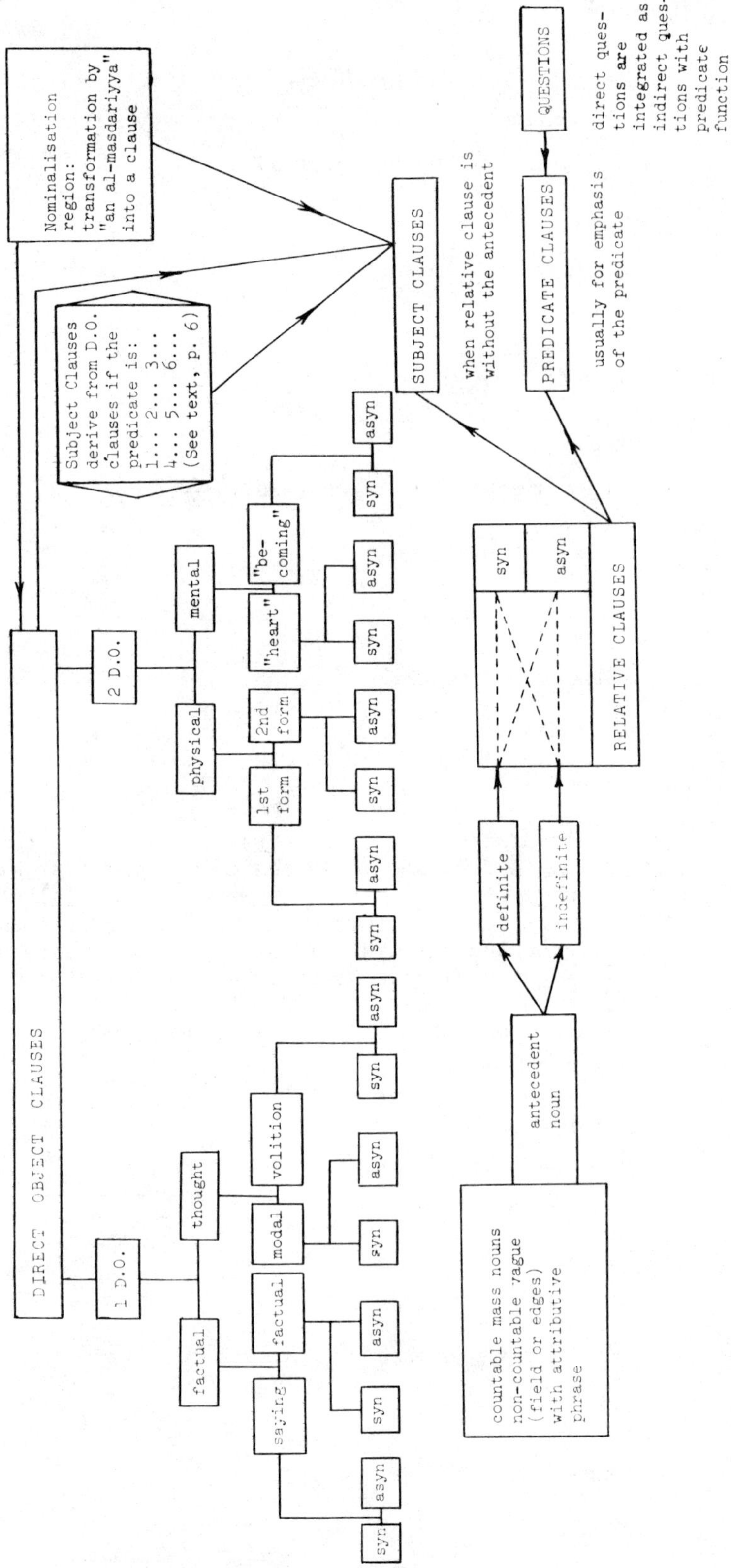

Fig. 3. Semantic Relations between some Clause Types

REFERENCES

ᶜAbd al-ᶜĀl, ᶜAbd al-Munᶜim. 1968. *Lahjat Šamāl al-Maġrib, Teṭwān wamā Ḥawlahā.* Cairo [in Arabic].

Blanc, H. 1964. *Communal Dialects in Baghdad.* Cambridge, Mass.

Blau, J. 1961. *A Grammar of Mediaeval Judaeo-Arabic.* Jerusalem [in Hebrew].

Blau, J. 1965. *The Emergence and Linguistic Background of Judaeo-Arabic—A Study of the Origins of Middle Arabic.* London: Oxford University Press.

Brunot, L. 1931. *Textes arabes de Rabat.* Paris.

Brunot, L., and E. Malka. 1937. "Proverbes Judeo-Arabes de Fès." *Hespéris* 24:153-81.

Cantineau, J. 1934. *Le dialecte arabe de Palmyre.* Beirut.

Colin, G.S. 1939, 1950. *Chrestomathie marocaine.* Paris.

Colin, G.S. 1957. *Recueil de textes en arabe marocain.* Paris.

Cowell, M.w. 1964. *A Reference Grammar of Syrian Arabic.* Washington, D.C.: Georgetown University Press.

Feghali, M. 1928. *Syntax des parlers arabes du Liban.* Paris.

Harrell, R.S. 1965. *A Basic Course in Moroccan Arabic.* Washington, D.C.: Georgetown University Press.

Kampffmeyer, G. 1908. "Texte aus Fes mit einem Text aus Tanger." *MSOS* 11:1-32.

Kampffmeyer, G. 1912. *Marokkanische Arabische Gespräche im Dialekt von Casablanca.* Berlin.

Marçais, Ph. n.d. *Le parler arabe de Djidjelli.* Paris.

Meissner, B. 1905. "Neuarabischen Geschichten aus Tangier." *MSOS* 8:39-97.

Mercier, H. 1945. *Grammaire arabe d'arabe parlê marocain.* Rabat.

Mitchell, T.F. 1962. *Colloquial Arabic, the Living Language of Egypt.* Teach Yourself Books.

Piamenta, M. 1966. *Studies in the Syntax of Palestinian Arabic* (Simple Verb Forms in Subordinate and Main Clauses of Complex Sentences). Jerusalem: The Israel Oriental Society.

Rosenhouse, J. 1974. "Coordination and subordination in urban Arabic Moroccan dialects." Doctoral dissertation, Jerusalem.

Rosenhouse, J. 1976. "The types of direct object clauses and their subordination in some colloquial Arabic dialects and Classical Arabic." *ZDMG* 126:10-24.

Saᶜid, M.F. 1955. *Spoken Moroccan Arabic.* Washington, D.C.: Georgetown University Press.

Singer, H.R. 1958. "Neuarabische Texte im Dialekt der Stadt Tetuan." *ZDMG* 108:106-25.

Spitaler, A. 1962. "Al-Ḥamdu Lillāhi Lladī und Verwandtes, Ein Beitrag zur mittel- und neuarabischen Syntax." *Oriens* 15-97-114.

Spitta-Bey, W. 1880. *Grammatik von arabischen Vulgardialekts von Aegypten.* Leipzig.

Van-Ess, J. 1917, 1971. *Spoken Arabic of Iraq.* London: Oxford University Press.

Van-Ess, J. 1918. *The Spoken Arabic of Mesopotamia.* London: Oxford University Press.

Weissbach, F.H. n.d. *Zum Irak-arabischen.*